◫ DORLING KINDERSLEY *READERS*

Level 2

Level 3

Level 4

A Note to Parents and Teachers

Dorling Kindersley Readers is a compelling program for beginning readers, designed in conjunction with leading literacy experts.

Superb full-color photographs combine with engaging, easy-to-read text to offer a fresh approach to each subject in the series. Each Dorling Kindersley Reader is guaranteed to capture a child's interest, while developing his or her reading skills, general knowledge, and love of reading.

The four levels of Dorling Kindersley Readers are aimed at different reading abilities, enabling you to choose the books that are exactly right for your child:

Level 1 – Beginning to read
Level 2 – Beginning to read alone
Level 3 – Reading alone
Level 4 – Proficient readers

The "normal" age at which a child begins to read can be anywhere from three to eight years old, so these levels are intended only as a general guideline.

No matter which level you select, you can be sure that you are helping your child learn to read, then read to learn!

LONDON, NEW YORK, MUNICH,
MELBOURNE, and DELHI

Art Director Cathy Tincknell
Publishing Manager Cynthia O'Neill
DTP Designer Jill Bunyan
Production Nicola Torode

Produced by Shoreline Publishing Group
Editorial Director James Buckley, Jr.
Art Director Thomas J. Carling
Project Editor Michael Teitelbaum
Designer Brandy Young

First American Edition, 2001
Published in the United States by
DK Publishing, Inc.
375 Hudson Street, New York, New York 10014
A Penguin Company

02 03 04 05 10 9 8 7 6 5 4 3

Library of Congress Cataloging-in-Publication Data
Teitelbaum, Michael.
    The story of Spider-Man / by Michael Teitelbaum.-- 1st American ed.
    p. cm. -- (DK readers)
    Summary: Relates the story of how the bite of a radioactive spider
turned Peter Parker into Spider-Man.
    ISBN 0-7894-7920-6 (lib.bdg. : alk. paper) -- ISBN 0-7894-7921-4 (pbk.)
    [1. Heroes--Fiction.] I. Title: Story of Spiderman. II. Title. III.
Dorling Kindersley readers.

PZ7.T233 Swr 2001
[E]--dc21

                2001017401

Color reproduction by MDP
Printed and bound in China by L. Rex

All illustrations courtesy of Marvel Enterprises, Inc.
Photography credits:
t-top, b-below, l-left, r-right, c-center
R.W. Jones/CORBIS: 15br
Hulton-Deutsch Collection/CORBIS: 17tr
Dewitt Jones/CORBIS: 20tl
Dorling Kindersley: 7tr, 10tl, 11cr, 11br, 12bl, 34 tl, 40tl

see our complete product line at

www.dk.com

Contents

DK DORLING KINDERSLEY READERS

PROFICIENT **4** READERS

THE STORY OF SPIDER-MAN

Written by Michael Teitelbaum

DK

DK PUBLISHING, INC.

A different super hero

A blue-and-red streak flashes across the night sky. A dark shadow moves among the city's rooftops. Who is this mysterious figure? It's the amazing Spider-Man!

Comic books featuring the exciting adventures of super-powered heroes have been around since the 1930s. But in August of 1962, writer Stan Lee and artist

Steve Ditko created a super hero unlike any who had come before.

Spider-Man made his debut that year in the Marvel Comics title *Amazing Fantasy*, issue #15. Spidey swung into the comics world, taking it by storm.

Before Spider-Man, all super heroes were practically perfect.

They were happy. The world loved them and appreciated their battles against evil. Nothing could hurt them, and they always saved the day.

Spider-Man changed everything. For the first time, young comic-book readers could follow the adventures of a hero who was more like them. Sure, he had superpowers, but he also had super problems. High school student Peter Parker, Spider-Man's true identity, was considered a nerd. He didn't have many friends. Most of the time he was lonely.

Even when he tried to do good, the newspapers called Spider-Man a menace and a villain. Here was a super hero who had real problems, like real people. He was an instant hit among readers. Comic-book heroes would never be the same!

But where did his story begin?

Major star
Spider-Man has starred in many comic titles, his own magazine, two animated television series, and a major feature film. There are tons of products bearing his image, as well.

Rockin' theme
The catchy theme song to the 1960s Spider-Man animated TV show was recorded by the rock band The Ramones.

Peter Parker, teenager

Peter Parker was one of the best and brightest students at Midtown High School. Unfortunately for him, though, he was not one of the more popular kids in school. He didn't have many friends. In fact, some kids at Midtown High often made fun of him.

One day, after school, Peter met a group of his fellow students.

"There's a new exhibit at the science hall tonight," Peter said. Science was his favorite subject. If

he wasn't reading a book, Peter could be found staring into a microscope. "Would any of you like to go with me?" he asked hopefully.

"Get lost, bookworm," sneered Flash Thompson, the school's football star. He shoved Peter aside, knocking his books to the ground. "Science hall. Hah! That's for losers. Let's get out of here."

As the others laughed and walked away, Peter knelt down and picked up his books. Then he walked home. Alone.

Microscope
A microscope is a scientific instrument which magnifies small objects. Doctors and scientists use microscopes to see things which can't be seen with the naked eye, such as blood cells.

Flash
One of the most popular students at Midtown High was Flash Thompson. Although he teased Peter all throughout high school, they became good friends later in life.

7

When Peter arrived home, his Aunt May was waiting. She greeted him with a cold glass of milk, some freshly baked cookies, and a warm, bright smile.

Peter lived with his Aunt May and Uncle Ben. They had raised him since he was a little boy, and he loved them very much.

"How was school today, dear?" Aunt May asked as Peter dug into the plate of cookies.

"Okay," he replied, shrugging his shoulders. Peter tried his best not to let the teasing of the other kids bother him. Some days this was harder than others.

That night at the dinner table, Peter's Uncle Ben brought up a subject he knew his nephew would find exciting. "Are you going to the new exhibit at the science hall tonight, Peter?" Uncle Ben asked. "It's supposed to be great!"

Top grades
Peter was the top student at Midtown High School in Queens, New York. He received the school's highest honors in science. Peter was a favorite among the teachers, if not the students!

Peter again shrugged and looked down at his plate. "I guess so," he replied. "None of the kids at school wanted to go with me."

"Well, I'll go with you, pal," said Uncle Ben, touching Peter gently on the shoulder.

"That's okay, Uncle Ben," Peter said smiling. "I think I'll just go by myself."

"Are you sure?" Aunt May asked softly.

"I'm sure," Peter replied. "And thanks. You guys really are the greatest."

Radioactivity
Energy given off by the nucleus of the atoms of some elements, like uranium *(above)*, is called radio-activity.

An unexpected bite

After dinner, Peter made his way to the science hall. There, a demonstration about radioactivity was about to begin. Peter looked on excitedly. Before him stood a huge machine. The machine hummed and glowed eerily.

A scientist stepped up to the front of the crowd.

"I will now demonstrate how we can control radioactivity, right here in the laboratory," he explained.

The scientist lowered the lights, then pressed a button on a control panel. Brilliant beams of radioactive energy streaked from one section of the machine to another. Peter and the others at the demonstration watched carefully.

No one noticed a small spider dropping from the ceiling on a nearly invisible web. The spider moved directly in the path of the radioactive beam. It was bombarded with radioactivity, absorbing the powerful energy.

Then the terrified spider leaped onto the nearest thing it could grab. It just happened to be Peter Parker's hand!

"Ouch!" Peter shouted, as the spider bit him. He shook his hand, and the spider fell to the floor, dead.

Spiders
There are more than 32,000 different kinds of spiders in the world. All spiders have eight legs, spin webs, and kill their prey with venom.

Arachnids
Spiders are not insects. They belong to a group of small animals called arachnids. Other arachnids include mites and scorpions.

WHAT'S COME OVER ME! I- I'M SCALING THIS WALL JUST AS EASILY AS I CAN _WALK!_

Sticky stuff
Among the many amazing things spiders can do is stick to any surface, using tiny claws on the ends of their legs. You may have noticed a spider crawling around on walls or the ceiling. This allows them to go almost anywhere they want!

"My hand! It really burns!" Peter shrieked. A powerful wave of dizziness rushed over him.

"Got to get some air," he moaned, stumbling out the door. When he was outside, Peter's whole body began to tingle. A feeling of power and energy raced through his arms and legs.

He was so shocked and confused that he stepped into the street without looking. A car speeding around the corner honked its horn and swerved out of the way. "Why don't you look where you're going!" shouted the driver.

Peter leaped for safety, and was shocked by what happened next.

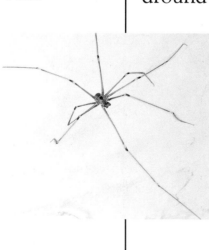

He found himself sticking to the side of a building, 30 feet up in the air!

"This is unbelievable!" he cried, as he scurried up the building to the roof. "First, I could sense that car coming before I even heard or saw it. Then I just climbed that building like a, well, a spider!"

Peter grabbed a steel pipe on the building's roof. The thick metal crumpled like paper in his fist. "How can this be happening?" he shouted.

Watch out! The car that almost hit Peter was not the first car to startle the young scholar. He often has his nose buried in a book as he walks down the street, not paying attention to where he is going.

Power revealed

The image of the radioactive spider biting his hand flashed through Peter's mind. "The spider!" he cried. "Somehow that spider has transferred its own abilities to me."

Even for a brilliant science student like Peter, this was a tough concept to grasp. He stared down at his own hands. His mind raced, trying to make sense of these strange events.

"I've got to find out what else I can do!" he exclaimed. Power surged through his body.

Peter leaped high into the air, doing several somersaults. He landed on his feet, then bounced up again as if the hard surface of the roof were a trampoline. Over and over he spun, jumped and tumbled, just like a champion gymnast.

"This is incredible!" he shouted, feeling like he could do anything.

Gymnastics
The sport of gymnastics requires great strength and balance. Young gymnasts train very hard to learn their spiderlike moves on various pieces of equipment, like the rings.

Peter next sprang into the air and landed on a thin telephone wire. He nimbly scampered along the wire, maintaining his balance perfectly as he ran.

"Just like a spider gliding along its web!" he exclaimed.

Secret identity
Even before he used the name Spider-Man, Peter realized the value of keeping his true identity a secret. He was worried that he might fail in his battle against Crusher Hogan. This led him to wear a mask for the wrestling match.

I've got to figure out what I should do with these unbelievable powers I've been given, Peter thought as he landed on the ground.

He spotted a sign outside a local sports arena. It read: "We'll pay $100 to anyone who can stay in the wrestling ring for three minutes with Crusher Hogan."

Here's a chance to really test my powers and make some money.

IT **WORKS!** I HAVE THE SPEED, THE AGILITY, THE VERY **STRENGTH** OF A GIGANTIC SPIDER!

HEY!

PUT YOU

Peter rushed home and put on some old clothes, including a mask to hide his identity.

Back at the wrestling ring, huge Crusher Hogan laughed when he saw the slender figure who had challenged him. "I'll try to make this as painless as possible," he chortled.

Peter swung into action. He vaulted over Hogan. Then he lifted the massive wrestler and climbed up a tall pole, holding Hogan with one arm.

"Put me down!" shouted the terrified Hogan from high above the crowd. "You win!"

Challenge
In the early part of the twentieth century, traveling carnivals featured wrestlers and boxers who challenged anyone in the audience to battle them in the ring. If the challenger could last in the ring for a certain amount of time, he won prize money. However, the performer usually won!

The costume

After the wrestling match, a television producer immediately rushed over to Peter.

"I'll pay you lots of money to show off your amazing powers on TV," the producer offered, handing Peter a stack of cash.

"You've got a deal!" Peter replied. *I think I'm going to like this spider powers thing!* he thought as he made his way home.

Over the next few nights Peter was busy in his room. He put his scientific knowledge to work creating mechanical web-shooters.

Amazing mask
Spider-Man's mask has special eye pieces. Like two-way mirrors, they allow him to see out but no one can see in. The mask not only hides Spider-Man's true identity, but also gives him a creepy look to frighten criminals.

When he wore them on his wrists,
Peter could imitate the web-spinning
ability of a real spider.

"I need a cool costume for my
TV appearance," Peter said. He got
busy creating a spider costume
complete with a web pattern.
He also invented a special spider
mask to keep his identity a secret.

"I guess I need to come up with a
good name for myself. I have spider
powers and a spider costume. I guess
I'll call myself... SPIDER-MAN!"

Webbing
The webbing in
Spider-Man's
web-shooters is
strong enough
to support his
weight as he
swings from
building to
building. It can
also form a
powerful shield
or be used as a
safety net or
even a
parachute.

USING HIS TECHNICAL INGENUITY, YOUNG PARKER
DEVELOPED DEVICES TO "SPIN" HIS OWN STICKY
WEBBING!

AND THEN, AFTER DESIGNING A
SUITABLY THEATRICAL COSTUME--

Under wear
Spider-Man's
costume is so
thin that he
can easily wear
it under his
street clothes.

19

One fateful night

The evening of Spider-Man's television performance finally arrived. The audience gasped in astonishment as he displayed his amazing spider powers.

First, he crawled straight up a wall. Then, pushing himself off, he flipped backward, landing on a thin tightrope. The crowd broke into thunderous applause.

Now I'll really show them something, Spider-Man thought. He fired a web strand to the ceiling.

Big top
At first, Spider-Man viewed himself almost like a circus performer who could use his power to entertain and make money. Many of his feats resemble superpowered versions of a trapeze act.

Then he swooped
over the audience,
just inches from
their heads.

The crowd gave Spider-Man a
standing ovation. A bright new star
had been born.

After the show, several people
who hoped to cash in on his talents
approached Spider-Man.

"How about an interview?"
asked a magazine reporter.

"Sign this contract!" someone
else shouted, shoving a piece of
paper and a pen into Spider-Man's
face. "I'll make you a movie star!"

*Nobody cared who I was when I
was just plain Peter Parker,* Spider-
Man thought. *Now everyone wants
a piece of me! I've got to think. This
is all too overwhelming!*

Dazzling
Whether
battling villains
or performing
on TV, Spider-
Man excited
those who saw
his incredible
powers in
action. Even
his webbing
dazzled
audiences with
its strength and
versatility.

Selfish?

Peter was never a selfish person. But after years of being picked on, his Spider-Man powers made him feel like he only needed to look out for himself. This selfish mistake would cost him dearly.

Uncle Ben

Peter and his uncle were the best of buddies. They went to the movies and science exhibits together. They even wrestled for fun. Uncle Ben was as much a father to Peter as his real dad. His death totally shattered Peter's life.

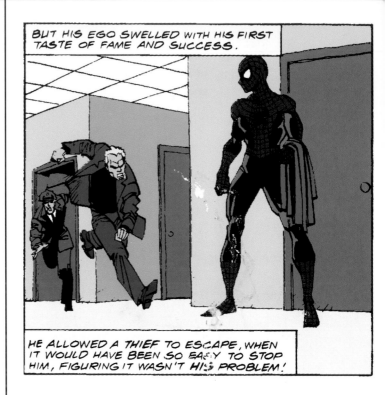

BUT HIS EGO SWELLED WITH HIS FIRST TASTE OF FAME AND SUCCESS.

HE ALLOWED A *THIEF* TO ESCAPE, WHEN IT WOULD HAVE BEEN SO EASY TO STOP HIM, FIGURING IT WASN'T *HIS* PROBLEM!

As Spider-Man paused in the hallway to think, a man raced past him. The man was closely pursued by a police officer.

"Stop that man!" shouted the officer. "He's a thief. If he reaches the elevator, he'll get away!"

Spider-Man stood by as the thief disappeared into the elevator.

"Why didn't you do something?" the officer asked. "You could have easily stopped him!"

"Why should I do your job for free?" Spider-Man replied. "You catch the criminals."

Peter returned home to the shocking sight of a police car in front of his house.

"Bad news, I'm afraid," the police officer said. "Your uncle has been murdered. A burglar broke into your house. Your uncle surprised him and was shot."

Peter stumbled backward. He clutched his head in disbelief.

"Uncle Ben, dead?" he cried. "No! It can't be!"

Aunt May
Still reeling with shock from the news of his uncle's murder, Peter raced into the house to find his Aunt May. A police officer informed him that his aunt was being comforted by a close friend and neighbor.

HE DISCOVERED HOW *WRONG* HE WAS DAYS LATER, WHEN HE RETURNED HOME TO FIND *POLICE* THERE. THE HOUSE HAD BEEN BURGLARIZED --

From that terrible day on, Peter promised to always take care of Aunt May. He worked hard to make enough money for both of them. Even after Peter married Mary Jane Watson, Aunt May remained a major part of his life.

With great power

Peter quickly put on his Spider-Man costume. Web-swinging from rooftop to rooftop, he swiftly made his way to a warehouse where the police had the killer cornered. Scrambling up the side of the building, he used his spider-strength to burst in through the roof.

"What?" shouted the startled criminal in alarm.

"There's nowhere you can hide from me!" Spider-Man announced. A burst of webbing snatched the criminal's gun away. Within seconds Spider-Man had captured the thief.

But when he took a look at the burglar's face, Spider-Man trembled in shock. This was the man who had run past him at the TV studio.

I should have stopped him when I had the chance, he thought. *If I had acted then, Uncle Ben would still be alive and here with me!*

Later, at home, Peter tried to comfort Aunt May.

"Oh, Peter," she cried. "How will we go on without him?"

As he hugged his aunt he realized the great lesson which would guide his life from that point forward—*with great power must also come great responsibility.*

On that day, Peter Parker truly became Spider-Man. He vowed to use his incredible powers to help others and to fight evil.

Great responsibiliies Peter went to work for the *Daily Bugle* newspaper as a photographer, while fighting crime as Spider-Man.

Spider-Man's powers

When Peter Parker was bitten by the radioactive spider he gained incredible powers. Just as spiders can stick to walls and ceilings, so can Spider-Man. Spidey also has amazing agility and balance. He can tiptoe on a tightrope, run while upside down, or bounce around a room like a rubber ball.

Spiders can lift many times their own body weight. So can Spider-Man. This helps him battle even the strongest super villains.

Web 'chute
Spider-Man can form his webbing into a parachute, allowing him to glide gently to the ground.

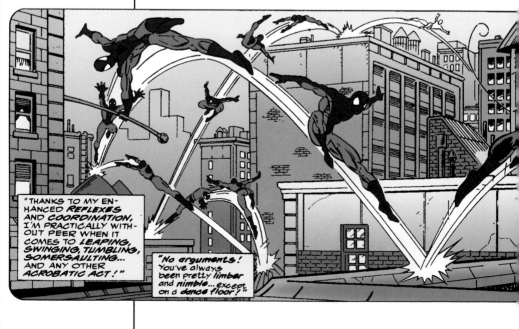

"THANKS TO MY EN-HANCED *REFLEXES* AND *COORDINATION*, I'M PRACTICALLY WITH-OUT PEER WHEN IT COMES TO *LEAPING, SWINGING, TUMBLING, SOMERSAULTING...* AND ANY OTHER *ACROBATIC ACT!*"

"No *arguments!* You've always been pretty *limber* and *nimble...except* on a *dance floor!*"

NO NEED TO RUSH, FELLAS! I'M NOT *GOIN'* ANYWHERE!

YES SIREE! THIS IS JUST WHAT THE DOCTOR ORDERED!

IN FACT, THIS IS THE MOST FUN A LITTLE SPIDER-MAN CAN *HAVE* WITHOUT LAUGHING!

When danger is about to strike, Spider-Man gets a tingling sensation in his head, seconds before the event happens. He combines this spider-sense with his speed, strength, and wall-crawling powers to escape even the most perilous predicaments.

Stuck like glue
Spidey also has a liquid form of his webbing, which forms an ultrasticky glue. Handy for stopping criminals right in their tracks!

Spider-Man uses his wall-crawling power to race up the side of a building.

27

Spider-Man's family

When Peter Parker was a baby, his parents died in a plane crash. He was sent to live with his Uncle Ben and Aunt May Parker. When Uncle Ben died shortly after Peter got his spider powers, it was left to Aunt May to raise him by herself.

Despite being frail and often ill, Aunt May was a loving, over-protective parental figure in Peter's life. She worried about him when he was late, fretted when he didn't finish a meal, and wanted only the best for her nephew. It wasn't easy raising Peter alone, but Aunt May worked extremely hard to make sure he had a good life.

As far as Aunt May knew, the biggest danger Peter faced in his teenage life was being late for school or not having many friends.

Reality check
Aunt May helps keep Peter grounded in reality. No matter how bizarre his life as Spider-Man becomes, his concern for his aunt's welfare reminds Peter of what is really important in life.

She believed Peter led a simple, sheltered life. Imagine how surprised she would have been if she had known the truth. That instead of studying at the library, Peter was often out swinging on webbing from rooftop to rooftop, battling super villains as Spider-Man.

Peter worked hard to keep his double life as Spider-Man a secret. He never wanted Aunt May to worry about him—at least not any more than she did already!

A strange proposal
In a strange twist of fate, Doctor Octopus, one of Spider-Man's worst enemies, once proposed marriage to Aunt May.

First love

Even though he dated Mary Jane first, Gwen Stacy was the first love of Peter's life. Tragically, Gwen was murdered by Spider-Man's archenemy, the Green Goblin.

Although Mary Jane Watson was not the first love of Peter Parker's life, she was his greatest love. Peter and Mary Jane first met after graduating from high school. They dated off and on for years. Mary Jane was very pretty and had a sunny, sparkling personality.

When Peter began dating Gwen Stacy, the first love of his life, Mary Jane dated Peter's friend Harry Osborn. But when Gwen tragically died at the hands of the Green Goblin, Peter and Mary Jane became a couple.

After high school, Mary Jane worked as a model and actress. Among other acting jobs, she appeared in the soap opera *Secret Hospital.*

As with most of the people he loved, Peter kept his identity as Spider-Man a secret from Mary Jane. Eventually, though, she discovered the amazing truth.

Once she knew his greatest secret, Mary Jane told Peter her own secrets. He learned that she had grown up in an unhappy household and that she had had a very difficult childhood.

This sharing of secrets brought Peter and Mary Jane even closer. Finally, in 1987, the couple married in a huge ceremony at City Hall in New York City. They then jetted off to Paris, France, for an exciting, romantic honeymoon.

"I NOW PRONOUNCE YOU HUSBAND AND WIFE!!"

Wedding bells
The wedding of Peter Parker and Mary Jane was one of the biggest events in comic-book history. The momentous union took place in *Amazing Spider-Man Annual #21*, released in 1987.

J. Jonah Jameson

A typical meeting between Peter and J. Jonah Jameson.

J. Jonah Jameson (known as JJJ) is the hot-tempered publisher of the *Daily Bugle* newspaper. Both Peter Parker *and* Spider-Man have had a strange and often stormy relationship with Jameson. But he has played a huge role in Peter's life, in both his identities.

After Uncle Ben died, Peter needed to earn money to help support Aunt May. He went to work as a freelance photographer for the *Daily Bugle.*

Peter's spider powers enable him to get spectacular shots from unusual angles. To Jameson's amazement, Peter is also somehow able to always get the best shots of Spider-Man in action. Jameson has no idea how he does this.

At the same
time that Jameson
buys photos from
Peter, he also runs
headlines in the
Bugle calling
Spider-Man a
menace. He claims

that the web-
swinger is a danger
to the citizens of the city,
complaining that the masked hero
takes the law into his own hands.

Ironically, Spider-Man has had
to save Jameson's life many times.
A number of Spider-Man's most
deadly enemies have attacked
Jameson and his family over the
years. Each time, Spider-Man has
swung to the publisher's rescue.

Although Peter's relationship
with Jameson is often difficult,
the grouchy publisher remains an
important figure in his life.

Robbie
Joe "Robbie"
Robertson is
the Editor-in-
Chief of the
Daily Bugle.
Robbie has
always liked
Peter, and has
even defended
Spider-Man to
his blustery
boss, Jameson.

Spidey shots
Peter captures
himself in
action as
Spider-Man by
hanging his
automatic
camera from
his webbing.

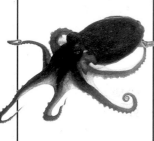

Multiarmed wonder

An octopus is a sea creature with a pouch-shaped body and eight muscular arms or tentacles. Each arm has powerful suction cups, which it uses to seize its prey. It then paralyzes the prey with a poisonous secretion. An octopus can be as small as two inches or as huge as 30 feet!

Greatest foes

The story of Peter Parker's life as Spider-Man began with a fateful bite. But for the story of Spider-Man—the super hero—you have to look to the greatest gallery of super villains any comic book hero has ever battled!

One of the super villains which Spider-Man has been battling the longest is Doctor Octopus. Named for the sea creature he resembles, Doc Ock, as he is called, didn't start out being evil.

Doctor Otto Octavius was a scientist who conducted experiments with radiation. In order to protect himself from the harmful rays, he wore four mechanical arms. These flexible arms allowed Octavius to work with dangerous chemicals and radioactive materials.

Then one day, a laboratory explosion changed the doctor's life.

He absorbed huge amounts of radiation which fused his mechanical arms with his body.

These arms were a part of him now and responded to his mind just like his real arms. They were incredibly strong and could hold anyone, even Spider-Man, in an unbreakable grip. Doctor Otto Octavius had become Doctor Octopus.

Since then, Doc Ock has tried over and over for world domination.

Goblin glider
The Green Goblin zooms through the air on a flying machine called the Goblin Glider. This flying wing is easy to control and can reach speeds up to 90 miles per hour.

The super villain who had the most impact on Spider-Man's personal life was Green Goblin.

Norman Osborn was a greedy man who owned a large chemical company. He tried to create a formula to increase his intelligence and strength.

Something went wrong and the chemicals exploded, almost killing Osborn. When he recovered, he discovered that the formula had indeed increased his intelligence, but it also made him insane. Putting on a creepy costume, he became the Green Goblin.

To make a name for himself among criminals, he decided to kill Spider-Man. First he created a chemical which dulled Spider-Man's spider-sense. This enabled the Goblin to follow the wall-crawler and discover his secret identity.

During their battle, an electric jolt caused the Green Goblin to lose his memory. Occasionally, the knowledge of Spidey's secret identity returned. During one of these times, the Goblin caused the death of Peter Parker's girlfriend, Gwen Stacy.

Hobgoblin
A man named Roderick Kingsley discovered the chemical formula that had changed Norman Osborn into the Green Goblin. Kingsley adjusted the formula to prevent the insanity that had overtaken Osborn. Donning a similar costume, he battled Spider-Man as Hobgoblin.

Sinister Six
Both Mysterio
and Vulture
joined Doctor
Octopus'
criminal gang,
known as the
Sinister Six.
The other of
Spidey's
enemies to join
were Kraven
the Hunter,
Sandman, and
Electro.

Other enemies

Spider-Man's trickiest enemy is
Mysterio, master of illusion. He can
vanish in a puff of smoke or create
the impression that there are 10 of
him surrounding Spider-Man.

Quentin Beck started as a
Hollywood stuntman. He soon
moved into the field
of movie special
effects. Beck
quickly became
one of the
most talented
creators of
movie
illusions in
the business.

But Beck grew tired of working behind the scenes. He craved the spotlight and decided that the quickest route to stardom was to create an identity for himself and take on a costumed hero—like Spider-Man!

Mysterio tried to convince the police that Spider-Man was a criminal by disguising himself as the web-slinger. Spider-Man foiled his plan, but Mysterio's career as a super villain had begun.

His skills have grown over the years. Mysterio is now a master of hypnosis, sleight-of-hand illusions, and explosives. He controls his opponent's senses, making them believe they are seeing things that really aren't there.

Mysterio once even convinced Spider-Man that he had shrunk to a size of six inches!

Vulture
Another super villain Spider-Man first encountered around the same time as he fought Mysterio was the Vulture. The Vulture uses an electro-magnetic flying harness which allows him to soar through the air and also gives him superhuman strength. Over the years, the Vulture has given Spider-Man some of his toughest battles.

Rhinoceros
A rhinoceros is a powerful hoofed mammal found in Africa, India, and Southeast Asia. It has one or two horns on the top of its snout. Rhinos are solitary, unpredictable animals with great senses of smell and hearing.

Like many of Spider-Man's toughest enemies, the super villain known as Rhino started out as an ordinary man. Although no one knows his real name, the man who became the powerful creature known as Rhino began his career as a small-time criminal.

Rhino on the rampage!

Because of his muscular body and low intelligence, he was selected by a team of spies to take part in an experiment. The spies used chemical and radiation treatments on the oversized hood, in hopes of creating a man with superhuman strength. What they got was Rhino!

His body grew in size and power. His strength and speed increased to incredible levels. And he wore armor made of a thick material as strong as a rhinoceros' hide.

Running at full speed, Rhino can smash through a building or crush a tank. He can even blast right into a mountain and come out the other side. Once he starts charging, Rhino is almost impossible to stop, even for a super hero with spider-strength and agility.

Kraven the Hunter
Kraven was a successful big-game hunter, but the prey he most wanted to capture was Spider-Man. Kraven drank rare jungle elixirs which gave him the speed of a cheetah and the strength of the strongest jungle beasts. It took all of Spider-Man's abilities to defeat this formidable foe.

Sandman
Career criminal William Baker was lying on a beach when a nearby nuclear reactor exploded. Radiation fused his body with the sand. As Sandman, he can change the molecules of his body into grains of sand, altering the shape of his body at will. This makes it very hard for Spider-Man to catch him!

The Spidey villain with the greatest worldwide influence is Kingpin. He may appear to be fat, but when you get close enough, you realize that his enormous bulk is solid muscle!

Wilson Fisk quickly rose to become the leader of organized crime on the east coast of the US.

Kingpin's web of crime extends around the globe.

Soon, his power spread worldwide and he was known as the "Kingpin of Crime." Eventually, those who worked for him and those who tried to stop him—like Spider-Man—simply called this mountain of muscle Kingpin.

Kingpin was always determined to be the best in whatever he did. He trained intensely in bodybuilding and person combat skills. He studied various martial arts and the Japanese art of sumo wrestling.

When his own enormous physical power is not enough (which isn't often) Kingpin uses his diamond-topped laser cane.

This combination of walking stick and weapon fires a powerful beam which can vaporize anything in its path. The cane also contains concentrated sleeping gas, which can quickly send any enemy to slumber land!

Electro
While repairing a power line during a storm, Max Dillon was struck by lightning. He survived and gained the power to control electricity—a power he chose to use for evil. Electric current surges through his body, and he can fire bolts of electricity from his fingertips!

Lizard
While operating on soldiers in the army, surgeon Curt Conners lost his arm. He created a serum in a vain attempt to make his arm grow back. A side effect was that in times of stress he changes into a giant lizard! Spider-Man tried to help Connors, but as the Lizard, he battled the wall-crawler.

Generally, Venom will never harm an innocent person but he makes an exception for Spider-Man!

Friend or foe?

On a far distant planet, Spider-Man found what he thought was a cool new look. A strange black substance oozed over his body and turned into a black-and-white costume. When he needed to be Peter Parker, all he had to do was think, and the costume changed instantly into his street clothes!

Soon, though, Spider-Man discovered that this was no simple costume. It was an alien creature trying to take over his body!

The creature hated loud noises. So Spider-Man went to the bell tower of a church, where the piercing chimes forced the shape-shifting alien off his body.

And that's where it found Eddie Brock. Brock was a down-on-his-luck journalist who had come to the church to pray. The alien attached itself to Brock's body, and the creature known as Venom was born!

Venom is especially dangerous to Spider-Man because he has all of the web-slinger's powers, plus more. Not only can he stick to any surface, use superhuman strength and agility, and form webbing, but Venom can change his appearance at will. Just by concentrating, he can make himself look like anyone he wants! He also can't be detected by Spidey's spider-sense!

Scorpion
J. Jonah Jameson was actually responsible for the creation of the super villain Scorpion. He paid private investigator Mac Gargan $10,000 to be the subject of an experiment in mutation. The experiment turned Gargan into a vicious, superpowered criminal.

The juggling act

Web-Slinger, Wall-Crawler, college student, photographer, husband, and nephew. Peter Parker/Spider-Man plays many roles in the juggling routine that is his life as a super hero with a secret identity.

It's a good thing he can web-swing across town in a hurry. Battling evil as Spider-Man would be enough of a full-time job. Add to that his responsibilities to do well in school and to earn a living shooting pictures (usually of Spider-Man in action) for the *Daily Bugle,* and it's enough to make anyone exhausted.

In addition, Peter tries to have a somewhat normal home life with Mary Jane.

College man
Peter Parker now attends Empire State University, where he studies science. Even when he is rushing to class, his spider-sense comes in very handy.

OH, GREAT! MY WATCH HAS STOPPED! I DON'T KNOW IF I'M LATE OR NOT!

WHOA! MY SPIDER-SENSE IS SIGNALING DANGER! WHAT COULD POSSIBLY--?

UH-OH! A LITTLE BURST OF THE OL' SPIDER-SPEED WILL PREVENT A NASTY IMPACT!

*Spidey swings
into action!*

He also always keeps an eye on
Aunt May, trying to find enough
time to spend with her. It takes
Spidey-strength just to stay awake
through all of those things!

This balancing act is what makes
Spider-Man unique as a comic-book
character. It's also what has made
him so real to readers and fans
around the world for so many years!

Nicknames
In addition to
"Spider-Man"
and "Spidey,"
this super hero
is also known
as "Wall-
Crawler,"
"Web-Swinger,"
"Web-Slinger,"
"Your Friendly
Neighborhood
Spider-Man,"
"Web-Head,"
and "Webbed-
Wonder."

Glossary

Adoring
Loving, admiring.

Agility
The ability to move quickly and precisely.

Appreciate
To see the good in, to have respect for.

Astonishment
Amazement, great surprise.

Bombarded
To be hit with.

Bulk
Large size.

Concentrated
Very powerful, increased in strength.

Crafty
Clever.

Debut
First appearance.

Domination
Total control over a person or group of people.

Editorial
An opinion expressed by the editors of a newspaper.

Elixir
A liquid potion, possessing magical powers.

Exhausted
Very tired.

Flexible
Easily bendable.

Instinctively
Automatically, without thinking.

Mechanical
Operated by using machinery.

Menace
Threat.

Orphan
A child whose parents are both dead.

Ovation
An outburst of applause.

Paralyze
To leave someone unable to move.

Predicament
A dangerous or difficult situation.

Pursued
Chased.

Secretion
A liquid which comes out of a plant or animal's body.

Sensation
A feeling.

Serum
A chemical formula.

Sheltered
Protected.

Sinister
Evil.

Sleight of hand
The process of fooling an audience by doing a magic trick involving skillful movement of the hands.

Slumber
Sleep.

Stuntman
Someone who does dangerous feats in a movie, filling in for the actor.

Swoop
Swing.

Thunderous
Loud, booming, sounding like thunder.

Trampoline
A net of strong canvas stretched across a frame, used for bouncing up and down.

Vaporize
To completely destroy until nothing is left.

Vault
To leap over something, using your hands for support.

Venom
A poison which comes out of the body of a snake, spider, or insect.

Index